Conversations With My Dog

Stephan Boden

(Translated version)

for

Nelson, Don, John-Boy, Willi
und Polly

Thank you!.

Polly is a female Parson-Jack-Russel. She was born in Hamburg, Germany in October 2006 and moved in with Stephan eight weeks later.

Her real name is "The Roadrunners Nessie", but as a sailor, Stephan did not like the name, which reminds of a famous sea monster. That's why she was named Polly on the very first day.

She is a 100%-terrier: always wide awake, fearless, inquisitive, very fixated on people and likes to make her own decisions. At the same time, however, she is well-mannered, very sweet, reserved, even rides the underground without a leash and masters city life with aplomb.

Since Stephan often sails with her on the Baltic Sea and writes books about it, Polly is considered "Germany's best-known sailing dog". She was introduced to sailing as a small puppy on a dinghy, and at the age of only six months she was already on a long sailing trip along the Swedish coast.

She loves people, hates cats and thinks that every day is a day full of adventure.

She has lived in Berlin for two years. Polly died in Dec. 2019, almost 1,5 years after I wrote this book.

Stephan was born in 1966 in Bielefeld, Germany.

He moved to Hamburg at an early age, where he tried his luck as an author and filmmaker.
In his childhood there were many animals in the house: dogs, cats, a goat, a pony, two horses, several parakeets and finches, a pheasant, many turtles and small ducks. His great love, however, is dogs. Before Polly, he already had four other dogs. A life without a dog is now unimaginable for him.
In his spare time, he enjoys sailing and has already written four books about it. The book "EinHundSegeln" is about life on board with Polly and won the ITB Book Award 2018.
In 2015, he met his current wife Anja and moved to Berlin to be with her. Stephan brought Polly into the marriage, Anja the tomcat "Dicker" - an 8-kilogram red tiger who is very headstrong, bites people and finds other animals strange.
Stephan attaches great importance to dog training, because a well-behaved dog makes life easier. However, in his opinion, this is only possible if you understand your dog.

Prologue

It must have been sometime in the mid-seventies. As a young boy, I go for an afternoon walk deep in the forest with my collie "Nelson". As I walk along a long forest path, Nelson pokes around in the undergrowth. In the distance I see a strange-looking man crossing our path. He disappears for a moment, but then comes back, looks at me and then walks towards me. I feel queasy. There are still about 150 to 200 metres between us. Slowly he approaches. I think about whether running away, stopping or walking on is the best solution. The queasy feeling turns into fear. The man stares at me. When there are only a few metres between us, Nelson comes out of the thicket and stands a few metres in front of me. He looks at the man and does not move. I stand still. The man continues to approach slowly but swerves to the side of the path. Nelson stands so that he is right between us. The man walks a wide arc around me, Nelson fixes him and continues to shield me. He moves so that he stays right between me and the man. Neither of us makes a sound. As the man disappears into the distance, the collie goes back into the forest. I still get goose bumps when I think back to that situation.

Until that day, the dog had always been a kind of cuddly toy for me, sometimes running after sticks in a funny way and often waking up in my bed in the morning. But this incident changed everything. I suddenly understood my dog as a partner, a close friend, a full-fledged family member. Since that day, I trusted Nelson with my deepest secrets, my worries and thoughts. He always had an ear for me. No death has ever affected me again the way Nelson's did. He was put to sleep years later because of massive hip problems. A world came crashing down for me. Two days later, we picked up a male mongrel from the shelter. Life made sense again.

Over thirty years and several dogs later, Polly came into my life. She is the most extraordinary dog I have ever had. And Polly is very communicative. One learns over time what looks mean, how to classify behaviour and what they are trying to say with some noises. Polly talks to me all the time, in fact whenever she's not sleeping. We understand each other's every word. She knows what I want, I know what she wants. She has a great sense of humour and for her, my silly jokes are mostly sensationally funny. Polly stands for what makes dogs so extraordinary.

Over time, I have learned a lot about dogs and experienced a lot from them. Dogs are the best teachers if you want to know how to deal with them.... You just have to listen to them. There are so many training methods nowadays - many of them are ineffective. Dogs know how to do it - regardless of breed, character or previous experience.

It takes a long time to trust a human 100%. A single second is enough to break this trust.
Dogs give their trust in a few seconds - and it lasts a lifetime.

This book is designed to help you understand dogs.

The Preliminary Talk

Polly! Here!.......................... Heeeeeere!
What's the matter?

Why do I always have to call you twice?
Do you call me twice? I don't get that at all.

I don't know. I call: "Here" and then I have to follow
it up with an angry undertone and a long drawn-out
"Heeere! Otherwise nothing happens. The same with
different "Sit" and "Down".
But you've always done that.

Because the fine dog doesn't listen the first time?
Yes! I always listen.

Okay - because you don't react the first time.
Should I do that after the first call?

That's the idea...
*Oh yeah? And how should I know? Since I've known
you, you've always said everything twice. So I*

naturally assume that the command has to be said twice for me to do it. If you say it only once, I won't even notice. I learned it that way. And I learned it from you.

Good to know. That's kind of true. But then you can do it the first time now.
Nope. Now I'm too old. I've gotten into the habit. Getting it out is a lot of stress for you and me. Let's keep it that way. That's the way it goes.

Sometimes you do it after just one shout.
I know exactly when! I's always when you shout it very loudly and insistently. Like on the street, for example, when a cyclist is coming. Then you shout "Sit!" in a very stern voice and I do it immediately. Because otherwise there's trouble. You should have thought about a uniform line beforehand. But take it easy: I always do what you say. I'm a very nice dog without any faults.

Hm... no, of course: without faults... Unless you're going completely crazy right now.
ME? When do I go crazy?

Shall I ring the doorbell?
Oh, I know what you're getting at. Because then I bark and jump around. What do you expect? That's what you've all been promoting.

Who "we"? "Promoted" how?
All the visitors! Whenever people come, they've always made a big fuss about me. They shout in high beeping voices "Helloooo Pollyyyyy", lifting me up, cuddling me and jumping and whooping. It's obvious that I'm going crazy. I'm stressing myself out.

Then don't do it.
No, my dear. Lessons learned are lessons learned - for the positive as well as the negative. You should have thought about that earlier. Besides, it's really unfair to always blame it on my race. "That's just the way they are" is the worst excuse for your own shortcomings.

Give me a break!
No, it's true. And your fault. Look at me: I'm also different out on the street, calm, obey well. Why do you say that? Because you showed me so. Or when we're on the boat: I'm totally relaxed and cool.

Why? Because you're relaxed and cool. I've learned a lot from the way you act. I'm a copy of your behavior. That's why you have to face it. It's not just at the door.

Tell me about it.
It really bothers me off when you yell at me and get mad when I bark and scream during applause. That's the way you taught me to act, too.

I did what?
Yes! You did! You used to take me to the stadium to watch football, even when I was a puppy. And then you always shout and cheer and clap. The more beer, the louder. And every time I joined in, you laughed about it and you did like it. Now you don't have to be surprised that I react like I do. So now when people clap at events, I just freak out. And I think that's nothing compared to you when your team scores a goal.

It's good that we talk openly.
Yeah, it's about time. Because you'll learn something from it.

Do you have other topics?

Thousands. How about you?

Ditto.
So what do we do?

Maybe we do it like this: everyone gets to name a topic in turn.
Okay. Who starts?

Always the one who asks.

***

Ball! Ball!

You've had a few dogs before I came. What were they like?

You don't talk about your exes.
Come on. I may be jealous, but I'm not interested in the past.

Oh, you know...I love dogs. I loved them all. Each in their own way.
But I think I'm right in assuming that none of them were as perfect as I was.

Your self-confidence is remarkable! But you're right. No dog was as special as you.
Because I have no faults! Because nothing about me bothers you.

Well...
We terriers know very well that we are the crowning of evolution.

You're very special for a crowning.
What do you mean, "special"?

Like when your brain stops working.
Huh? What do you mean?

Shall I show you?
Please.

Hold on, I'll get something....
Loo, what will happen to you if I show you this?

*BALL! BALL! BALL! BALL! BALL! BALL! BALL!
BALL! BALL! BALL! BALL! BALL! BALL! BALL!
BALL! BALL! BALL! BALL! BALL! BALL! BALL!
BALL! BALL! BALL! BALL! BALL! BALL!*

That's exactly what I mean.
*BALL! BALL! BALL! BALL! BALL! BALL! BALL!
BALL! BALL! BALL! BALL! BA...*

Polly! Stop it! Stop it! Don't! No! Stop it!
*BALL! BALL! BALL! BALL! BALL! BALL! BALL!
BALL! BALL! BALL! BALL! BALL! BALL! BALL!
BALL! BALL! BALL! BALL! BALL! BALL! BALL!
BALL! BALL! BALL! BALL! BALL! BALL! BALL!
BALL! BALL! BALL! BALL! BALL! BALL! BALL!
BALL! BALL! BALL! BALL! BALL! BALL! BALL!*

BALL! BALL! BALL! BALL! BALL! BALL! BALL!
BALL! BALL! BALL! BALL! BALL! BALL! BALL!
BALL! BALL! BALL! BALL! BALL! BALL! BALL!
BALL! BALL! BALL! BALL! BALL! BALL! BALL!
BALL! BALL! BALL! BALL! BALL! BALL! BALL!
BALL! BALL! BALL! BALL! BALL! BALL! BALL!
BALL! BALL! BALL! BALL! BALL! BALL! BALL!
BALL! BALL! BALL! BALL! BALL! BALL! BALL!
BALL! BALL! BALL! BALL! BALL! BALL! BALL!
BALL! BALL! BALL!

Off now! I'm taking it away now.
BALL! BALL! BALL! BAL..Where is the ball? Where is the ball?

Sit!
But, but where is the ball?

That's enough now, isn't it?
Is it in your pocket?

Off! Do not start!!!
BALL! BALL! BALL! BALL! BALL! BALL! BALL!
BALL! BALL! BALL! BALL! BALL! BALL! BALL!
BALL! BALL! BALL! BALL! BALL! BALL! BALL!
BALL! BALL! BALL! BALL! BALL! BALL! BALL!
BALL! BALL! BALL! BALL! BALL! BALL! BALL!
BALL! BALL! BALL! BALL! BALL! BALL! BALL!
BALL! BALL! BALL! BALL! BALL! BALL! BALL!
BALL! BALL! BALL! BALL! BALL! BALL! BALL!
BALL! BALL! BALL! BALL! BALL! BALL! BALL!
BALL! BALL! BALL! BALL! BALL! BALL! BALL!
BALL! BALL! BALL! BALL! BALL! BALL! BALL!
BALL! BALL! BALL! BALL! BALL! BALL! BALL!
BALL! BALL! BALL! BALL! BALL! BALL! BALL!
BALL! BALL! BALL! BALL! BALL! BALL! BALL!
BALL! BALL! BALL! BALL! BALL! BALL! BALL!
BALL! BALL! BALL! BALL! BALL! BALL! BALL!
BALL! BALL! BALL! BALL! BALL! BALL! BALL!
BALL! BALL! BALL! BALL! BALL! BALL! BALL!
BALL! BALL! BALL! BALL! BALL! BALL! BALL!

BALL! BALL! BALL! BALL! BALL! BALL! BALL!
BALL! BALL! BALL! BALL! BALL! BALL! BALL!
BALL! BALL! BALL! BALL! BALL! BALL! BALL!
BALL! BALL! BALL! BALL! BALL! BALL! BALL!
BALL! BALL! BALL! BALL! BALL! BALL! BALL!
BALL! BALL! BALL! BALL! BALL! BALL! BALL!
BALL! BALL! BALL! BALL! BALL! BALL! BALL!
BALL! BALL! BALL! BALL! BALL! BALL! BALL!
BALL! BALL! BALL! BALL! BALL! BALL! BALL!
BALL! BALL! BALL! BALL! BALL! BALL! BALL!
BALL! BALL! BALL! BALL! BALL! BALL! BALL!
BALL! BALL! BALL! BALL! BALL! BALL! BALL!
BALL! BALL! BALL! BALL!

***

Intellect vs. Instinct

Last night I noticed something again that makes me wondering ever since I got dogs: When I leave the room, you don't react. But when I leave the room to leave the house a bit later, you react. Then you look at me and want to go with me.
Of course I want to come along. I always want to go!

I know that, but that's not the point. I ask myself: How do you know I'm about to leave the house?
You show me that.

It can't be. Because even if I don't have my shoes on and I'm not wearing a jacket, you know that beforehand. You also know far in advance that we're going to the forest later, for example, or on holiday.
As I said before - you show me that.

That's just it, it can't be. Yesterday I left the room about twenty times throughout the day. I said nothing to you ten minutes before I left the house, behaved as I always do and gave you no sign that I was leaving.

You show it to me anyway.

But how?

Part of my answer would only unsettle you.

Come on. Tell me! There's a trick to it.

It's something you humans don't understand. You have no instincts. You're so numb that you don't notice what's going on around you. That's why so many people have trouble getting along with their dogs. You hardly know anything about our abilities, what we can do and how we read situations. You perceive the world completely differently than we do. You perceive much less. Sometimes I laugh when I see how dull you go through life.

I once read that you can smell a person's condition. Because the skin relaxes or tightens and that changes the smell.

No, that alone is certainly not it. It's an interplay of all the senses and instinct. We smell, hear, see, but we also have instincts. You don't have that. You don't even have real sense organs.

Well, I have ears, nose, eyes and mouth too.
That thing on your face doesn't deserve the name "nose". It's not a sense organ on you. That thing doesn't work at all.

At least I can smell when you fart.
Terrier farts - the best of all farts! But that's about it. When I see you bending over a meal and getting really close to smell it. I'd still be able to smell it in the neighbour's house across the street.

I know that you can smell incredibly well.
Do you know how I can tell that you don't even begin to understand how good we can smell? I get that a lot. Many people approach dogs by holding out the back of their hand so that the dog can smell the person in peace. It's so funny and stupid. I can smell them twenty metres away. When they come towards me like that - that's so funny. But it also confuses me. Some dogs get scared of it.

So the nose is the secret?
It's only a small part. You just don't get it. You know, you're always so proud of your intellect, but

that ruined a lot of things. You're always thinking, you're totally cerebral. You make assumptions and often draw the wrong conclusions from what your atrophied sense organs can still produce. If you put on a jacket, that doesn't mean for me that you're going out of the house. If you put on a jacket because it's cold, I notice that. I know you're cold. But any human being would ask: "Oh! Are you going out?"

Nothing is safer than instinct. It never betrays you. With us dogs, it's a mixture of emotion and instinct. With humans, emotion and intellect. Emotion and intellect, however, are often competitors, that is why your instincts no longer work. You lost it.

I recently read an article about assistance dogs. These dogs accompany diabetics, for example, and show them in time when they are hyperglycaemic or hypoglycaemic. They know exactly what the human's values are and react immediately. Can you do something like that?

Of course I can. I know all that. I just have to be trained to react to what is specifically desired. That's why there are drug dogs, cash dogs and other search dogs. They are specialised. Normal dogs just pick out what is important for us.

When I come home and I'm in the hallway, you almost always respond. Even if I walk very quietly. Can you smell me?
No, I can feel you. I know that's you coming in. But I don't know if it's the special sound when somebody turns the key, the smell or whatever. I just know it. Instinct is much more than you think. You have allowed these abilities to atrophy over time. When you were hunter-gatherers, you could do that too.

Hm. So the question is, what is better? Intellect or instinct?
You can't have both together. But it's okay that communities of purpose like ours form as a result. Otherwise we probably wouldn't get along so well. So I'll continue to look out for you.

Oh, yeah. You could let me know at the next party as soon as I reach my alcohol limit.
You don't need me for that. Everybody can see it in the way you walk.

26

***

Pack

By the way, we have a little hierarchy problem in our pack.

You think so? I think it's clearly regulated here.
Between us, yes, but not with me and Anja.

You have a problem with Anja?
No! I love her. But her place in the pack is not very clear.

Well, since you're at the bottom of this hierarchy, it's actually clear.
I don't see it like you do.

Polly, you and I have been together for 12 years now. Anja is my wife and absolutely on the same level with me. Even though she came along much later.
You may see it that way, but that's exactly our problem.

No. In the end, you have to bow to what I see as...
You don't understand.

Then you explain it to me.

.

So. You are the clear leader here for me. Then comes me and then comes Anja. It's a classic social system called a pack.

Polly, you come after Anja.
And that's the problem: A pack is an evolved system. The alpha dog, the pack leader, goes ahead. Then it goes according to strength and assertiveness, and there come the middle dogs and at the end the weakest, who run behind the pack, turn around and look out for potential dangers. Everyone settles this system among themselves.

But then everything is clear. Anja gives you the commands and therefore she is clearly ahead of you in the hierarchy. Besides, she is stronger than you.
She's weaker! She does everything I want.

She's never had a dog either and falls for your sweet and sad faces. But in the end, I decide for you where you stand.
And that's not how it works. The alpha dog doesn't care who falls in line behind him. Only if someone

wants to dispute his position, he will intervene. So you can't determine how it works with Anja and me.

Interesting. And what should we do to put Anja in front of you?
She has to assert herself and be clear. She has to lead me, not me her.

And that's okay with you?
Since I'm not such an alpha dog and don't aspire to the top.... yes - that would be okay.

In a way, you dogs are weird.
Just because we're not like you doesn't make us weird. Listen, here's the thing: we dogs need a clear structure. We need clear hierarchies and pack leaders to guide us. If we are left too high in the pack, it often doesn't work out well. We can't do anything with equal partners, it confuses us.

What could Anja do?
For example, not to put up with so much from me. Then, by the way, she can also control me very well with the food. She decides when to give me food - not me. At the moment, I always get something when

I push her. For example, when she comes to me on the sofa, she can scare me away and I have to look for a new place. She always has to show me: Polly - I'm the boss here for you. If she does that consistently, I'll always line up behind her. She could also, for example, always go through the front door in front of me. Not just now and then. But as it is, I'm always a bit confused because you just take sides with her and you're constantly trying to regulate our positions. It drives me crazy. That's our job. When you're away, everything is different here. Then I'm the boss, protect her, growl at other men and look after her.

You never growl at people.
Not when you're around. Then I would only intervene if someone attacked you. But I watch out for Anja when we're alone.

Okay, I'll talk to her. It won't be that easy because, as I said, she has no experience. I think we have to practice a lot.
Be glad I'm not an alpha dog. That would be difficult. An alpha dog needs very clear instructions and a very strong leadership. Otherwise it won't

work. It's not like with those crazy cats. That's all Anja ever had before.

Hm...
Yes?

I'm not sure if you're not an alpha dog, too, when I think about your training phase. After our boat trips, when you are allowed to do much more than usual, I always made - I call itn"asshole week", where you don't play, you don't pet, you don't walk without a leash and I'm even stricter than usual. If I don't do that, you dance on my nose after every vacation.
Well, that's more due to the breed. We terriers - the best dogs there are, by the way, did I mention that? - use every space we can get. If you explain that to Anja, I'm sure she'll know what to do.

The Tomcat

Do you actually feel comfortable at home?
Yes, I do, but you know what I really think sucks?

No.
That I'm only ever allowed in the living room.

Otherwise you'd kill the cat. So we have to separate
you physically.
It's your own fault.

What did the cat do to you? Why is it his fault?
It's not the cat's fault. It's your fault.

I'd like an explanation.
*Do you remember when we sailed to Sweden when I
was little?*

Yes, of course.
*We used to go out in the morning. And there were
always so many cats at the fishermen's houses.*

Yes, but none of them hurt you.

And why were you always so happy - at least you laughed - when I chased them away?

Because I thought it was funny that you were into it. *You told me to go after her.*

Told you? Me? Never ever, Polly.
You did. Who else? Don't you remember that you used to point at the cats and then say in such a hissing tone "Polly, there! Cats, cats!"? That was the sign for me to hunt. And if you then laugh and are happy, that confirms my behaviour.

You're not serious?
I am! The tone of voice is exactly the one you use when you throw a ball and then say "Go Polly! Go catch it!" with such a sharp, hissing sound. What else am I supposed to think but to chase the cats?

Hm. Let me guess: And now it's too late to train you out of it.
You're a fast learner! Well, it would work - but you don't have that much patience.

Oh, that's annoying. Can't you just let it go?

Well, I can't help it if you marry a woman who brings a cat into the marriage.

Well, then it'll just be: your realm is limited to the living room.
Great. How old is the cat?

A bit older than you. We don't know exactly. They say it's about 14, 15 years.
And how old do these suupid monsters get?

I don't know. The oldest cat lived 38 years and 3 days.
That's f***d up.

What are you gonna do?
Let me go to him and the problem is history...

Listen! It's a living creature, just like you.
You can be very insulting. That bitch has nothing on my class. When I hear that stupid "meow-meow"...

You're unfair.
Nothing has the class of a terrier! Nothing.

I won't say anything about that now. Besides, it's Anja's cat, her heart is set on him.
And why does he keep biting her? And why does he bite her all the time? And why does she always cuddle with me instead of him?

Because he's a tomcat and some tomcats are sometimes a little crazy.
I told you, they're stupid bastards.

Look, I'm not discussing this. We tried it for a long time with you two, but it doesn't work. You're always going crazy.
Because he provokes me. And because you raised me that way. You used to love it. Besides, you hardly make any effort with us.

Why? After all, you've sat in a room together before.
No, that's not enough. You have to do this every day. You can't stop. You'll get there eventually.

You think so?

When you're in the room with him and you're paying attention, yes!

And if you're alone in the room with him?
I'LL KILL HIM!

***

The City

Why do we always have to walk around in the city?
Can't we just go into the forest all the time?

Well, we just live in the city. Speaking of which -
how do you actually like Berlin?
What? What is Berlin?

Well, Berlin, where we've been living for two years
now.
Is it any different than before?

You don't know the difference between Hamburg
and Berlin?
All I know is that we live in a different flat and with
Anja. And the stupid tomcat.

Funny.
What's funny about it?

Berlin is a completely different city. You don't
notice that?
We used to take the underground less. And the
scooter thing is new, too.

Do you actually like riding the scooter?
It's great to ride. But the backpack is stupid. Because I'm not allowed to look out.

When it gets warmer in spring, you can do that. In the cold, you'll only get conjunctivitis from the wind.
Okay. I feel like I'm trapped. You can hardly see anything through this stupid net. But the eyes thing is bullshit. I run around in the cold. Nothing happens.

But you don't run as fast as the scooter.
How fast is it?

Well, it's allowed to go 30 mph, but it's going 50.
Ridiculous!

You're so full of yourself. But back to Berlin. It's funny that you don't see it as a different city. Let's say we were to walk out of the front door here and then Hamburg would suddenly be downstairs. Wouldn't that irritate you?
Nope.

And suppose we were to walk out of our front door here and instead of Berlin there was suddenly a forest or a harbour in front of the door.
And?

That is so crazy..
I don't worry about things like that. I don't know where we'll get off if we take the bus somewhere. You worry about that. All I know is that we always go to the seaside on this one train.

I thought you could tell where you were by the smell....
When I go to great places I know, I can smell it beforehand.

But you can't smell the difference between Hamburg and Berlin?
Nope. Not really. Because it doesn't interest me.

But what do you think of our new hometown then?
Well, the same as always. Sometimes great, sometimes annoying. I think it's great that there's

*always something going on here. There's so much to
see and smell.*

And what's annoying?
Escalators.

I don't understand that. In the subway station you
jump on by yourself and like it. But at H&M you're
such a bitch.
*H&M? Is that the narrow escalator in the shop with
the carpet in front?*

Yeah, you don't like them, huh?
Because someone stepped on my paw there once.

On the escalator?
Yeah, when he was squeezing by.

I don't remember that. I didn't even notice.
You don't notice a lot of things.

Do you think so? I think so.
*No. You always have your eyes up there somewhere,
I'm down there and always have to walk around
between someone's legs. Nobody pays attention to
me. Yesterday, someone hit me on the platform with*

a wheeled suitcase. You can't imagine what my situation is like down there.

Hm. But I can't always carry you.
No way. But you could keep a closer eye on what's going on around me.

But I always do.
There's a lot of room for improvement...

Okay, I'll pay more attention. Have you had any more bad experiences like that?
No, but I'm always scared when you tie me up in front of the supermarket,

I only do it in the supermarket that's in the mall. And I always tie myself in big knots to scare off any thieves. I know it is a problem and I never have a good feeling about it. But sometimes it has to be that way. And I look out at you all the time too.
But you don't notice the kids who annoy me sometimes. Recently a boy kicked me.

Kicked you?
Yes, he came close to me with his mother and kicked me in the side.

Hm. What should I do?

Just don't take me with you.

But...

Listen. You bought me at some point. You have responsibilities. I'm not a stuffed puppet animal. Just because you're too lazy to walk me the 2 minutes home, you put me in danger and constantly expose me to situations I don't like. One day you'll come out of the shop and I'll be gone. You know full well that everyone thinks I'm cute and I'd go with anyone.

You're right. I'll stop.

Fine.

You know what? I'm tired. Let's talk more tomorrow.

Absolutely. I haven't finished talking about the city yet. Can I have another treat?

Nope. You're getting too fat.

I'm glad you're watching my weight, but you don't seem to care about yours.

Dog-Waste-Bag-Stories

Do you know what I want most of all?
My figure?

I wish that one day you'd start taking your piles not on green spaces but deep in the bushes.
What makes the difference?

The difference is that then I won't have to pick up every turd you make.
Come on, it's not that bad, is it?

Look, you're about to be 12 years old. Every day you poop an average of three times. That means I've picked up your piles about 13,400 times. I'm always standing behind you and have to pick it up. It often stinks.
Why don't you leave it?

If I leave your piles, others will too. If I take it away, I set a good example and others pick it up too, if necessary.

What kind of bourgeois are you all of a sudden?

Man, Polly. Think about it. If everyone leaves their dog turds lying around, other people will get mad. Mad at dogs. There's so many dog haters anyway. And what's the reason for that? Untrained, fearful dogs and dog shit on the street. The result is strict dog laws or maniacs who put out poisoned bait. You have to suffer from that. You can see it now in Berlin: now leashes are compulsory everywhere. Because some dogs just cause stress or people are annoyed by dog poo.

Hm. But that's not because of the dogs. Is it so bad to pick up my poop? They're good terrier poo. The best piles there are.

Well, it's not gonna be my hobby. Apart from the fact that you really do place considerable stink bombs for such a cute little animal, I wouldn't mind much. But there are sometimes situations you don't want to experience.

My breed is considered very curious by nature, so I ask for the stories about that.

We once had a date in the evening to watch a Champions League match with friends in a pub. On the way there, you took one of those mushy super-turd on a grassy area next to the bus stop. As usual, I pulled the bag over my hand and wanted to remove it. When I reached in, I thought, "This feels different now than it usually does." By then it was too late. The bag had a flaw: it was not sealed at the bottom, but open. So I reached straight into the pile. Then the bus came. I got on with you and had to ask the driver to buy a ticket. Try pulling your wallet out of your pocket with one hand, taking out change and paying. I couldn't wash my hands until I got to the pub.

I can't help that. That's human error.

Not entirely. Because that day you ripped off someone's food again. That's why it wasn't one of those usual rock-hard kibbles. That wouldn't have been so bad.

So please. The manufacturer of the bag has failed and so have you. You check a bag like that beforehand. I don't feel responsible.

I have other stories: I once took you to pick up a friend from the airport. When I was in the building, she texted me that she was waiting outside for a cigarette. The two of us went for a walk beforehand

and passed dozens of green spots. But what do you do? When leaving the terminal, in the middle of the revolving door, you put your slogan in the middle of the grooved carpet in the revolving door! Before I could react, the door came with this little broom below and spread your pile out nicely. It looked like in a crêperie. Also that day you ate some crap on the street, like a leftover kebab or something.
Ooops! What did you do?

Nothing, I f****d off.
It can't have been that bad.

Yes, it is, and most of the time it's bad because you always have to eat crap like that.
Man! There's a lot of good stuff lying around. I'm a dog! I have to eat it.

I can understand a leftover kebab. But not when you eat dune grass on the beach and a day later your poop is hanging out of your butt on a piece of dune grass. I then have to pull a long piece of dune grass out of the pooper of a hysterically screaming dog on the street.
Oh yes, that was bad!

Not for you at all. You're just making a fuss. I, on the other hand, kneel in the middle of the street between people, push down a wildly kicking and squealing dog and pull things out of its butt. It's degrading, embarrassing and sometimes you have to explain it to strangers because they think I'm torturing you.

Listen. You decided to get a dog, so don't whine now if you have some negative experiences. You are responsible for me, for better or for worse.

Besides, what could be nicer than having terrier droppings on your fingers? Because that means: you, dear Stephan, have the incredible luck to be allowed to be together with such a great creature. Isn't that just great? Apart from that, such stories are great, because without them your life would be terribly boring. But this way you always have something to tell. Important for a book writer...

I hate you.
Why do you hate me?

Because you're right.

Primary School

Was it actually hard to raise me?

It was hell on earth!
Why is that?

Well, you're a terrier...
Dude, we are sooo awesome. We are the best!

..and that alone does not make parenting easy.
Because you have a very strong will.
That's what makes us.

I agree, I don't like boring dogs. But still, it's really
hard to tell you what to do.
But I obey.

Well, we wouldn't pass a companion dog test.
What's wrong? What's the problem?

Just take this morning when I forgot the leash: The
command "stay" only lasts a few metres, then I have
to repeat it - sharply - so that you don't run ahead.
Not only that, but you always wait very eagerly for

my "And run!" You interpret every little movement of mine as if you could start running now. That's why I can't even look at you, because then you think: that's it - I'm running. I'm not even allowed to clear my throat!

I just wanted to go home and eat quickly. You can also let me run ahead. I know the way.

No, it's clear. And then you run ahead and when you get to the door, the stupid neighbour's dog comes and you don't get on with him.

It's not me, he's an unsocialised idiot.

But even if I let you run ahead. Don't you realise you can't eat until I get there?

No, I don't think that far ahead. I live in the "here and now".

You see! That's why my job is to think ahead and order you around.

And what was so hard about teaching me that?

If you had been an ugly, fat dog with an overbite, I could have handled it better. But you're so small, sweet, sooo cute and so gentle.

Yeah, it's awesome, isn't it?

That's what comes with it: You cute little monsters know that! And you use it as a weapon against us. You know very well that it is difficult for us to give such cute little furry animals the hard
hand. Consistency suffers from this. And without consistency towards you, you're lost.
But we're really cute, aren't we?

You're cute little buttcrackers. Cute monsters. At night you lie snuggled up under the covers and during the day you send my life to hell.
So nice!

You've caused so much pain to so many people.
Why is that?

Because visually you are exactly what single, older women want. They see you and think: "Oh, what cute little animals, so cute. I'll get one of those for my old and lonesome days." And then at some point they notice what's wrong with you and so the poor grannies have such little yapping, far too fat monsters at their side for 15 years or more. They don't expect that.

You can read about how to deal with us everywhere.
Besides, there are dog schools.

...Hm, that's clear. Dog schools whose names end with "y" and whose logos always feature a colourful paw. Do you remember that we went to one of those? With a friend who we accompanied with her Parson Russell?
Yes, of course.

And how was that?
Ridiculous. Absolutely child's play. They would never have been able to handle me. What happened to the other Parson, anyway? He went there for years.

I've seen him. He's wearing a muzzle.
Poor guy.

That's why your breeder never gives you to people who have no dog experience. And you don't need to give her a poodle history either.
Well, a poodle would certainly be quite unsettled by the strict upbringing.

Is that a complaint?

No, not at all. I need clear guidance. In other words, someone who tells me where to go. We are, after all, pack hunting dogs. We are bred to go into the foxhole and there we have to make our own decisions. And that's what we always want: to decide for ourselves. But that would not work well in the city. That's why it's good that someone like you goes out in front and makes the decisions. If that wasn't the case, a car would have run me over long ago or I would have run away. Especially in the city, I'm happy not to have to decide anything. I would be completely lost. Besides, I would get into trouble with you.

Do you think that's stupid?
That I do what you say?

No, that I'm so strict.
No, not at all. If you weren't so strict, I'd be all over you. You know how it is with those treat dogs.

Treat dogs?
Yeah. Those dogs that only come because there's treats. They only obey when they feel like it. They don't realise how serious the situation is.

They don't realise the gravity of the situation. You say that? Wouldn't you prefer to get a treat when you obey instead of being told off when you disobey?

Listen, are you stupid? Where do we come from? We are dogs! We live in packs with clear hierarchies. No one gives a treat to anyone else. There's trouble if you don't play by the rules. What have you seen more often? Dogs that bitch at each other? Or dogs that reward each other?

Stupid question, of course you only see bitching.

Of course you do. Because that's what works. I don't have anything against rewards, but that's not enough as the only means. You can do that in between, but not as motivation.

Don't I give you enough treats?

Yes.

I don't understand. You just said that...

You don't understand, do you? I'm a dog! I love to eat. I eat till I drop. That's why I love treats. But if you used that as a training tool, it wouldn't work. You know, when there's a cat walking across the *street, I think that's a lot more appealing than a f***ing treat. Then I run over and chase the cat. I would then say to myself: "It doesn't matter if it's a treat, I get them all the time anyway - now it's the cat's turn!"*

But since I know I'll get into terrible trouble, I don't do it. It's as simple as that.

When I live in a pack, I also don't go to the food of my "superiors". Because otherwise there's trouble.

Besides, I'm not a Border Collie who is crazy about giving commands. You can also give him treats. Or Labradors and other food-controlled breeds. I am a terrier!

Lower Creatures

What do you think of me as a master?
I still don't understand how it could have come to this.

How what came about?
That you're my master.

It's very simple. I picked you up at the breeder's. Since then you've been my dog. And I'm your master.
I don't mean that. I mean, what qualifies you to be one in the first place.

Apart from the fact that there is no qualification - apart from this dog licence - I already had many dogs before and therefore had enough experience.
You don't understand anything. Actually, I should be your boss. So purely from the point of view of logic.

Interesting thesis. However, it always makes sense to support theses with well-founded arguments.

Look, for 3.9 billion years, ever since the first organisms were called "life", living beings with inferior abilities have been telling those who are superior where to go. Yes, you humans have achieved much and are the rulers of life. You tame animals, ride horses, train elephants, breed pigeons and clone sheep. That's all well and good. But we dogs, for example, have only been oppressed by sheer force. Darwin would order things quite differently and put you in line behind us.

You know it when you get so tired all of a sudden?
You can't stand the truth.

Where are you dogs so superior to us?
In almost every way.

Is that so? I want examples.
We run faster, we are stronger, we have better senses, the better antennae, we hear frequencies you don't even know that they exist. We can see in the dark, we can orientate ourselves by smell, we can read tracks. Our fur saves us clothes, we...

Stop!
Had enough?

No. I'd like to get into this. Start slow.
Okay. We can run faster than you.

You wanna race? You against me? Anything goes: bike, scooter, car.
That doesn't count. Aids are unfair.

Just because you can't drive a car, scooter or cycle, it's not unfair.
Yes, it is. Without your scooter, you don't stand a chance against me. And not without your bike either. Even with a bike you can hardly beat me. Just face it: If you don't have one of those, you're screwed.

And you without your nose.
It's not an artificial aid!

Okay, that's true. But otherwise you also benefit a lot from our human achievements, right?
Pfft. Which ones? It's all to make up for your physical deficiencies.

Oh yeah? Well, tomorrow I'll try to get that new food bag of yours open without a knife or scissors.
Give it to me, I'll bite it open.

Good idea! Maybe you'll get rid of your tartar with it. It's pretty sharp-edged, that packaging. Then I won't have to drive you to the vet with the scooter (aid), who will then anaesthetise you (aid) and clean your teeth with scratching tools (aid).
I don't care if the tartar has to be removed. It's nonsense.

No, it isn't. Meanwhile, your mouth smells like a cow in the back, middle. And eventually you'll get a toothache, and that's even worse.
You're using disease to distract yourself.

No. But without all these tools, your life would look a lot worse. Even your dry food is made by machines.
Pfft, then I'll go hunting. It's more humane anyway.

Where do you want to go hunting? At the train station or in the shopping centre?
In the forest!

And in which one? And how will you get there?
I'll find one.

Great. On the way there you'll be hit by a bicycle, then a motorbike will run you over and a car or a bus will do the rest.

Without you humans there would be forests everywhere and no roads.

Without us humans you wouldn't even exist, no one would ever have bred your race. And even if you did exist, you'd still be sleeping in the forest. You're a coward. And I want to see you, if you see a rabbit now, how you want to catch it and even if you catch it, you little food diva certainly won't eat it.

This is your fault.

Oh, yeah? Why is that?

Because you didn't raise me right.

Great. Should I have moved you into a cave? Then you'd have to go hunting every morning to get something to eat. But I would have taken the hunted animal from you and eaten it myself. You would have been left with the bones and innards of the hare.

Yuck.

No sleeping in the bed. You can lie on a f***ing rock.
As if you and Anja could stand not having me in bed with you. I'm laughing out loud! You want it too.

You can't be species-appropriate in the city. Especially not in flats.
Well, you could give it a try.

Like that "Natural Dogmanship" thing? The Waldorf School for Dogs? Would you like that? Maybe I'll start peeing and marking in the flat.
Don't say anything against marking - it's a very good way of communicating.

But it has one crucial flaw.
Which one?

Well, as a bitch, you pee sitting down. But do you know why male dogs lift their legs?
Of course they do! So that the next dog thinks you're taller if you pee higher up. That's very clever of us.

But it cancels itself out because everybody does it. Every dog makes itself bigger. Where exactly is the advantage now?

I'd like to go outside now, please. I have to pee.

Good, then the lower creature, your pack leader, puts on his shoes and gets the leash, right?

Terrier Existence

What breeds did you have before me?

Well, I grew up with a collie. Then came a few mixed breeds, including a husky mix, and then came you.
What were they like?

All different. From calm to hectic. They all had their own idiosyncrasies. They were all very sweet. None of them as crazy as you. That's the terrier behaviour I mean.
I am not crazy, our breed is considered a working terrier. I'm alert, I'm bright and I like to have chores. I'm dutiful.

And sometimes you have a roofie. I wonder to this day why the Reverend John Jack Russell, when he bred your breed, didn't work on a few finishing touches.
Because we are perfect!

Do you think it's perfect to kill yourself?
When do I kill myself?

Last year, for example, when we were on the beach at the baltic sea. At some point you had the idea of getting stones out of the water by diving for them with your head.
That won't kill me!

Is that so? At some point, when I was swimming in the water myself, I saw you holding your head under the water and tugging. There was a stone stuck too tightly in the bottom. You couldn't get it loose. But you had to have it. Instead of surfacing and breathing, you pulled and pulled and pulled. I ran to you, which takes a really long time in the water, and then lifted you out. You were breathing fast like a fish. If you didn't have your white fur, I'm sure you would have turned blue. I'm sure you would have killed yourself.
I don't remember that story.

I know! That's why you did it again the very next day.
But it's good that you explain it to me. Now I know.

And what would you do differently next time?
Ahem, nothing? WHEN I WANT A STONE, I GO FOR IT.

See? That's what I mean. Do you think that's normal? You'd die just to get a stone?
Yeah, sure.

Polly, the whole world is full of stones. Then just take another one.
You don't understand. It's not about just any stone. It's about this particular stone.

What is sooo special about this one stone that you should give your life for it.
It's just: THE STONE.

Okay, let's say it's the most special stone in the world, worth dying for....
You're on the right track.

... so, THE STONE!, as you call it. Why, when you have pulled it out, are you no longer interested in it afterwards? You spit it into the sand, forget it and then fetch the next stone out of the water.

Because the next one is also THE STONE.

That's what I mean by terrier roof damage.
Just because it's too high for you doesn't mean you have to believe it's an evolutionary or even a breeding flaw. You just don't follow me intellectually.

Oh, you think so? Next example: you once fell down a cliff because a stick slipped over the edge. You jumped down after it. A ten-metre cliff!
Guess why...

Because it was THE stick?
You're a quick learner!

This is really too high for me. Wait - I've got something else.
What?

Fox!
WHERE? WHERE? WHERE? WHERE? WHERE?

See?

WHERE? WHERE? WHERE? WHERE? WHERE?
WHERE? WHERE? WHERE? WHERE? WHERE?

Heeeellooo, Pooollyyy.
What?

How you freak out when I say "fox"...
WHERE? WHERE? WHERE? WHERE? WHERE?
WHERE? WHERE? WHERE? WHERE? WO?WO?
WHERE? WHERE? WHERE? WHERE?

Stop!
What? Why?

How can you have the stupid idea that there's an F**
running around in this kitchen.
A what?

A FOX
WHERE? WHERE? WHERE? WHERE? WO?WO?
WHERE? WHERE? WHERE? WO?WO? WHERE?
WHERE? WHERE? WO?WO? WHERE? WHERE?
WHERE? WHERE?

Stop it! Holy moly! Isn't it awful to be a terrier sometimes?

Nah, it's totally awesome. Terriers are the biggest, fastest and best dogs in the world.

Darling, you're weight is 5.3 kilos and fit into a burlap bag. You're small.

I don't think so. And true size doesn't show itself that way.

But you have to admit that you are a very small dog.

I am not small!

You see - this view alone shows me that you're completely insane! If I had to describe what's going on in your heads, I would say: In one half of your brain children's music is permanently playing, in the other Rammstein is permanently playing and in the middle there's constant noise, like a drum solo.

Wow! You've described that pretty well.

Do I have to take you to a psychologist?

What's a psychologist?

A doctor for the head.

I hate doctors.

Stomach Stories

Why do you hate the vet? He always tries so hard and is very nice.
Because he always pokes me.

I'm sorry, but you have to be vaccinated regularly. And it's not that bad. After all, he gives you liverwurst out of a tube at the front when he gives you a shot at the back.
It's not just the poking either. I hate that he's always pressing on my belly and fingering my fanny.

It's your own fault. You brought all these stomach problems on yourself.
Why?

Well, how can you eat wet sand on the beach in large quantities? That's really stupid.
I was thirsty.

Mm, sure. And half an hour before, you wouldn't drink the water I offered you.
I was thirsty all of a sudden!

Oh yeah? Even when you ate dune grass once? The next day I had to pull whole stalks out of your back.
They got in the way when I was looking for the ball.

Do you know what you've had come out the back? Once a whole rubber band! And if you eat leftovers with chilli peppers in them as you walk past a Mexican restaurant, you really don't have to be surprised about stomach problems.
But that was also delicious!

For the 300 bucks I left at the doctor's for that alone, I could have bought you better things.
If you'd done that, I wouldn't have eaten the chillies.

You eat till you drop. You're never full.
I was full once.

I remember when I came home and you'd raided your food box. You looked like a pear and couldn't walk. The next day at the doctor's you weighed 7.5 kilos instead of 5. Luckily my measures were effective, otherwise the treatment would have cost a lot of money.

Why was that so bad?

Well, some of that huge amount of dried food had got stuck. It couldn't get out. The doctor said, that he would have to operate if it didn't come out the back within 24 hours. So I gave you two jars of sauerkraut. And you even ate them in your condition.

So?

Have you ever seen an elephant pile?

That bad?

Yes.

But other than that, I'm perfectly healthy, right?

Yeah, totally. Except for this spondylosis.

What's spondylosis?

It was discovered in an X-ray when you had another stomach thing. It's an ossification of the spine.

Is it gone?

No, you can't get rid of it.

There's nothing you can do?

Not really. The doctor said that you can't tell when the first symptoms will appear. It could be in two years, but also sooner or later. The only way to delay it is to let you run around less. Fetching balls and things like that.
And what do we do now?

Nothing, we go on like this. I think it's better to let you have six years of fun than to let you have two years more and not have any fun. That's why you can continue to run, jump, climb and swim as before.
You know what?

What?
I think that's good.

***

Dogs

I would like to talk to you about other dogs.

Oh! A nice topic.
You know that curly-haired mongrel from down the street?

The one with the woman who always has those silly stuffed bears dangling from her backpack?
Yeah, that's the one.

What about him?
I feel so sorry for him.

Why do you feel sorry for him? I think he is annoying. The wife too, by the way.
It bugs me how he is going crazy when we approach. A hundred metres before we get there, he either lies down flat on the road in anticipation or jumps and pulls on the leash. Why did the woman teach him to do that? Doesn't she know that? The poor guy. He thinks every dog encounter is something special.

The woman says he's just so impetuous. There must be something - hold on - "wild in the mix".
I think there's something stupid in the woman's mix.

I know what you're getting at.
It's true. Look at her. As soon as she sees us - the same with other dogs, by the way - she opens her eyes and says in her disgusting squeaky voice: "Ohh, look, there's Pooooollyyyyy again!" She must realise how she's cheering the dog on. And when I walk past completely unimpressed and full of ignorance and he pulls wildly on the leash and turns, she always talks so loudly to him. Doesn't she realise that this stresses him out? And makes it worse?

No, most people don't notice that. Besides, we have to talk about people rather than dogs on this subject.
I suppose so. Why do so many dog owners notice...

..most, Polly, most...
... okay, most dog owners don't actually realise that they've completely spoilt their dogs?

Oh, when you talk to them, they always say things like: "it's the breed", "he's just like that", "he has a trauma from puppy days"....

... "he doesn't do anything, he just wants to play"...

If you shout that, it means that the dog is running uncontrollably towards another person or dog and scaring the other person. Only that point is enough to make you think about yourself and your dog.

Like that aggressive white shepherd dog in the neighbourhood

Exactly. And you know what the best thing is?
Tell me!

Do you remember Jackie, who used to run around there? The one with the harness that said "Riot" on it?

Oh my God, he was so annoying.

His owners told me at some point that they were now going to a dog school. I asked them which one. And here's the thing: the woman with the untrained white German shepherd had been going to a dog school for years and she recommended it to them because it was "really super". You have to think about that! They let a school be recommended by a woman whose dog doesn't obey at all.

I'm glad we moved away from there.

Well, yeah. In relation to other dogs, it's no better here.

Do you think it's difficult to train dogs?

No, not at all. It's so easy. I mean, you just have to look at a pack of dogs and see how dogs interact with each other. Then you know how to train.

Yes, I know. We need clear messages, a clear line, consistency and someone to follow. And it's true that we are very simple. When I see how complicated you people are.

We, on the other hand, are very simple among ourselves. Only your human behaviour sometimes makes us complicated. I have an example: This poodle from the side street, do you know which one?

I think I do. The one with the silly jacket. The one that gets so crazy around other dogs.

Yes. He does that because when he was a puppy, his owner used to pick him up when other dogs came. Since then he knows that other dogs are a dangerous situation.

She says he's just an alpha male.

No, he's insecure. He just learned that way. Other dog = danger. Simple formula. When he was a puppy, she should have just let him handle it on his own. But she always had to intervene because she was afraid.

But it's almost impossible to talk about it with people like that. There are always excuses for everything and at some point they get angry. But you have to ask yourself why people should be different when dealing with dogs than when dealing with people.

Are people like that with each other?

Often, unfortunately.

Wow, I am so glad I'm a dog.

Wireless

How do you actually feel about having to walk on a leash?
It's OK. Sometimes I even think it's great.

Really? When?
For example, when I'm unsure. At the main station, for example, when it's particularly crowded.

And what do you like about the leash?
It gives me security. I'm in touch with you and don't have to worry about where I'm going. I have enough to do with looking after all the legs and feet that swarm around me. It's a relief to be on a leash.

And what else?
Well, I never think it's bad. Well, it would annoy me in the forest or something. Because then I want to run. But in the city it's okay. I also notice how you relax then.

Sure, because then I don't have to pay so much attention to you. There are always cyclists on the pavement or cars coming out of driveways or something.

Am I actually allowed to walk without a leash in the city?

To be honest, I don't really know. The dog laws change all the time. But I don't think they have recently.

Anyway, as I said, I don't mind.

It used to be different.

Yeah, when I was little.

That was about the biggest job I had in terms of parenting. Just how long some walks took. Horror.

Why? I don't walk slowly.

Nah, but to stop you pulling on the lead and walking under tension all the time, I always stopped. Because that's the trick. So to stop whenever you pull again. Then you stand still until you take a step back and the leash is without tension. Only then do you go on. The purpose of this is to show you: If

you pull on the leash, exactly the opposite of what you want happens.
Did that work?

It took so long to get there. Because as soon as I started walking again, you pulled again. Then I stopped again. And so on. And you know what was even worse and took even more time?
Tell me!

Change of direction. Because when I realised months later that it does not really works fine for you because you're a terrier....
Such perfect dogs!

...I then changed direction. So as soon as you pulled again, I went in exactly the other direction. Sometimes it got so wild that I could only make up about a metre in ten minutes. But that worked out well.
I'm glad you did it that way and not with such a rolling line.

That's the worst thing ever! A dog never learns to walk on a leash with those things. How could they?

Or they are dogs that don't obey and people use that as a way out, so that the dog can move at all.

But that's stupid for the dog. Do you know why? He no longer knows what a real leash is. He then has a walking radius of ten metres and doesn't know the difference between walking freely and walking on a leash. I always know what's going on when you put me on a leash. That's why I think these retractable leashes are terrible. Those things in combination with a harness - that's tantamount to surrender. That's surrender before leash walking. The dog never learns that with it.

Some people say a harness doesn't put so much pressure on the neck when the dog pulls.

Listen, we are dogs. We are not stupid. We already know that once we stop pulling, it doesn't hurt the neck. All a harness does is make it easier to pull. Then you just keep going.

And what do you think of these drag lines?

They seem to be modern. We never used one. But it's similar to the clothesline you used to tie around me to practise commands. So it's good for training. But not forever. Some people use them all their lives. These dogs often run wild on the leash. They are modern, but in my opinion that's all. Being modern is modern.

Well, yes - but it looks more like the successor of the retractable leash - only that it looks more "professional", because many people use it as a training leash.

So again, it's a tool as an excuse for one's own failings. Do you know what's annoying about both types of long leashes? That many dog owners can't handle them. They let their dogs run on this long leash, and other people have to get out of the way. We've even almost crashed into a retractable leash with our bike. If you use a leash like that, you have to use it properly and watch your dog at all times and keep in touch with it.

That's always the problem: it's not the dogs, but the owners.
Maybe we should turn the tables and make the dogs the pack leaders. We instinctively do less wrong.

How right you are!

Perspective

Why is it that I never get anything from your table and others always want to give me some of their food?

Because other people fall for your looks.
And you don't?

No, I know the intention behind it. And if I fell for it all the time, you'd look like a liverwurst by now. Do you actually know how you look in such situations? So you say to yourself: "I'll put on my sad, sweet look"?
No. But I've tried out many different looks for a long time. When I look like that, the chances of success are high. So ears up, eyes open and turn your head slightly.

That means you don't know what effect it has on other people? That they get pity?
No. If I found out that I had to put on an ear or turn in a circle or bark, then that's what I would do. I

don't care what people think - the main thing is that I get something.

I was once sitting in a café, you were tied to the chair and joined the next table. After a while, an elderly lady says to me, "You have to give your dog something to eat, he looks all sad."
That is entirely your problem. I am not sad at all. And I don't look sad consciously. I just make a face that you obviously interpret as "sad".

To make matters worse, if you then wag your tail very slightly when you make eye contact, people become even softer.
That works great! People who are stubborn can be grabbed in the end. The wagging works really well.

You always read from behaviourists and dog experts that dogs have no consciousness.
Oh, you know. These behavioural experts say something different every week. They don't really look that deeply into us. Besides, it's also a form of consciousness, because I'm aware of what's successful and what's not. So in principle I already know quite well what works and what doesn't.

Something else that I read again and again, but which is completely different from what you do, is television. You often hang around in front of the TV. But one reads again and again that you don't even recognise what's going on on the screen.

Huh? What do you mean: why do I immediately run in front of the TV when I see a cat or a mouse?

They say you react to the sound and only see a few moving lines that move.

And why do I run to see a cat without a cat sound in a music video?

Maybe because the colourful lines look so great.

Rubbish. Because I see the cat. If it was only the sound that mattered, I wouldn't run around the room looking for the antelope that just ran across the screen from right to left. If you observed it carefully, I also ran to the left. And let's be honest: the sounds of antelopes really don't excite me - because I don't know these sounds at all.

But then what do you like about the stock prices that always run on a strip at the bottom of the screen on news channels?

Well, I always wait for one of those numbers to fall out of the side of the TV at some point. AND THEN I GO AND GET IT!

You only watch TV sometimes. When do you actually feel like it?
When I'm not busy. On days when we've been swimming or running around outside for hours, I would never have the idea of running to the TV. So when I'm glued to the telly again, you know what to do.

Well, sometimes it's quite handy if you sit in front of it for hours reading CNN stock quotes.
I've noticed you always turn that on before you leave the house and go away for a while. Why do you do that?

Wouldn't you like to know? Nah, I'm not gonna tell you. Cause if you figure out tricks, they don't work.

Errors

I would like you to enlighten me. I have lived with dogs for 50 years. In the last few years, there's been such a big fuss about the training and behaviour of dogs. Dog schools have alternative concepts, dog trainers appear on TV in rows, they even fill whole stadiums with visitors. What strikes me is that there are always new theories about dogs.
Which ones would you like to have explained?

Let me start: Well, I know tail wagging as an expression of joy. But now you read again and again that it is excitement. Is that true?
Have you ever seen me excited and wagging my tail?

No.
You see. Well, it happens. But most of the time, it's pleasure. You know how it is: when you say funny things, being silly, I'm happy. Or when I'm half

asleep and you mention Anja's name. I'm not excited, I'm happy. Sometimes there are situations when I meet another dog, for example. Then I don't wag out of joy either, but rather out of a kind of tension. But you can tell, because then the tail only trembles slightly. There are certainly dogs that wag even when they are not happy, but you can recognise the condition more from the overall behaviour.

Good. Then I once read in a textbook about your breed that you shouldn't look dogs deeply in the eye because it scares you.
Huh? Nonsense. I stare at you all day and also expect you to return the stares to make contact with me. If you don't look at me, you're ignoring me. Nah, I think that's bullshit.

And then I read somewhere that dogs can't have a guilty conscience because morals are foreign to you.
You're reading the wrong stuff. Let me ask you a question: When I've done something that I know I'm not allowed to do, how do you know? How do you often notice that?

Well, like when I come into the room and you're sneaking around in front of me and throwing yourself down. Like the other day when you raided the bin.

I know I'm not supposed to do that. I know I'm not supposed to do that. And I know there's gonna be trouble.

Okay, that's not remorse, that's just fear of being told off.

What's the difference?

Well, remorse comes from within. You realise it was a mistake and you're sorry.

Then I know remorse.

When?

Well, when I'm too dominant towards Anja. I've already growled at her twice, then I immediately jump on her and give her a friendly lick on the nose. Is that what you call remorse?

Yes, something like that. But there I have the next topic: licking noses. Many say this is dominating behaviour. Is that true?

Listen.... dominate you?

Well, maybe not me, but Anja, for example.

I have a different grip on her. Leave it. No, I'm not a dominatrix. It's love.

Good, I'm reassured. One more thing: hunting instinct: you're a hunting dog, too. Is the hunting instinct really that strong?

Nope. I've never hunted.

But they say you can't turn off the instinct in hunting breeds.

If you'd let me go after the rabbits before, I'd go after them now. But since you've forbidden me to do that before, I'll leave them alone.

Running rabbits don't excite you?

No, why should they? Since I was never allowed to run after them, I've got rid of this attraction. Why should I run after anyone for no reason? Listen..: I always hear people saying: "Oh, Sparky is like that - it's just his hunting instinct". But the owners often encourage it. It has become fashionable to lay tracks in the forest to keep the dog busy. Of course, as a dog you start to develop these instincts.

I have often wondered about that. Funnily enough, real, trained hunting dogs also obey the hunter. Despite the hunting instinct.

Do you know what I think? Many dog owners who have not trained their dogs properly and who are always running away use this hunting instinct as an alibi. They use it to excuse their own failures.

Well, I'm glad that you don't have such alibis.

Huh? There are plenty of excuses from you why I do some things. You often blame it on race, but actually it's upbringing.

What?

Yes.

Tell me. Say what?

Never ever! I won't tell you secrets that give me freedom. Besides...

Let me guess: It's too late anyway.

I like how teachable you are. Almost as good as me.

Honesty

Did you ever have a time without a dog?

Yes, a few years. That was completely unnecessary.
Why was that?

Heinz Rühmann, a famous german actor, once said: "A life without a dog is possible, but pointless." I fully agree with that. For me, life without a dog is dreary. I can't even imagine what it would be like without you. I think we live really well together.
Yes, every day is an adventure and it's often very funny.

So you know humour?
Of course, you should notice that. For example, I find it very, very funny when you say silly things. There is a certain tone of voice that really makes me curl up in laughter.

You can't really tell. Of course, when I talk to you like that, I notice that your tail is propelling wildly, but there are all kinds of theories about tail wagging.

Leave out all the crap you read on the internet and concentrate on what you see.

I would also interpret it as you think it is funny.
Yes, very.

So, a lot of things are funny for you?
Yes, almost everything. I love to ride on the bike, if you put me in the burlap bag or backpack, that's very funny, boating too, parties, somehow I think, it is all very exciting and great.

I'm amazed at how you always go along with it all without a problem. Just put it in your backpack and that's it.
If you hadn't started doing everything with me when I was a puppy, I would certainly be different now. The second day after I arrived, we went on the underground, cycled and in the evening we went to a party.

Many people told me that maybe it was too much.
No, not at all. That was fine. I'm simply used to everything. Nothing really shocks me.

Do you remember how you freaked out when I took you to the city on your first New Year's Eve as a little puppy to show you fireworks?

I love fireworks! If you hadn't taken me then, I might be afraid of them now. No, it was quite good that you showed me everything straight away.

And aren't I often too strict?

Don't worry about that. As I said, we need clear instructions and above all consistency. How strict and unyielding do you think the alpha dog is in a pack of dogs? You're a joke compared to that. We can handle it.

What do you find most important in living together?

Loyalty and honesty.

Hm. When I think about it, it's really the case that you dogs are all very loyal.

Without loyalty it doesn't work. Otherwise a pack like that would break up. There would be murder and manslaughter - just chaos. But I also expect this loyalty from every member of the pack.

Am I loyal?
Most of the time.

What? When aren't you?
Just one example: sometimes you're distracted and don't realise what my needs are. It sometimes happens that you sit at the computer and write very concentrated. If I then have something - for example, I have to go out urgently - and I report it, you sometimes send me to my basket in a huff. You don't pay any attention to me. You're just annoyed by me. But it doesn't work like that. You chose me, so sometimes you can't just ignore me and take advantage of the fact that I obey you.

Hm.
It always happens when you're worried about something. You're in your own world. Do you remember that situation on the boat when I was scratching that box and then you were yelling at me to stop?

Yeah, I remember that. You were so annoying.

I was thirsty. The bowl wasn't there, otherwise I would have scratched at it as usual. You would have noticed that. So I scratched the box where you keep the water tank. But instead of thinking about what I wanted, at some point you grumbled because you wanted to read your book.

I'm glad you're so honest about that.

I'm always honest. Dogs can only be honest. Dogs, unlike you humans, can't lie.

I know that. That's why in my next life I think I want to be a dog.

Yes! A terrier! The best dogs! Soo cool!

Oh Polly... I love you!

Can I have a carrot or maybe a radish?

End.

Impressum

Conversations with my dog (translated from german)
Stephan Boden
All rights: Stephan Boden

Responsible for the content::
Stephan Boden
Wilhelmsdorfer Straße 71
14776 Brandenburg an der Havel
Germany

mail@bodensbuecher.com

Printed in Great Britain
by Amazon

29825244R00066